T0039215

CALM *is* *the* WATER

A Guide to Inner Peace

GEORGE E. SAMUELS

iUniverse LLC
Bloomington

CALM IS THE WATER
A GUIDE TO INNER PEACE

Copyright © 2014 George E. Samuels.

All rights reserved. No part of this book may be used or reproduced by any means, graphic, electronic, or mechanical, including photocopying, recording, taping or by any information storage retrieval system without the written permission of the publisher except in the case of brief quotations embodied in critical articles and reviews.

iUniverse books may be ordered through booksellers or by contacting:

iUniverse
1663 Liberty Drive
Bloomington, IN 47403
www.iuniverse.com
1-800-Authors (1-800-288-4677)

Because of the dynamic nature of the Internet, any web addresses or links contained in this book may have changed since publication and may no longer be valid. The views expressed in this work are solely those of the author and do not necessarily reflect the views of the publisher, and the publisher hereby disclaims any responsibility for them.

Any people depicted in stock imagery provided by Thinkstock are models, and such images are being used for illustrative purposes only. Certain stock imagery © Thinkstock.

ISBN: 978-1-4917-3037-9 (sc)
ISBN: 978-1-4917-3036-2 (e)

Library of Congress Control Number: 2014905705

Printed in the United States of America.

iUniverse rev. date: 03/31/2014

DEDICATION

ONE LOVE OM!

Quotes

"The highest good is like water.
Water gives life to the thousands of things and does not strive."
–at Wu Dang Mountain, China, Nov. 2012.

Inner Peace, Like Water, Seeks its Own Level

—G.E. Samuels

CONTENTS

INTRODUCTION

Are you at peace? Do you stay calm and relaxed in stressful situations? Are you really at peace? We need to ask ourselves these questions while we let the answers lead us to a better understanding of what life means. Most people are concerned, but not enough to spend a moment actively evaluating whether they are at peace; but some feel the need to be at peace, to turn away from all the turmoil, have ample time to relax, and have a sense of calm in their lives.

Calm is the Water explores the idea that we all deserve to be calm, stress free, happy, and at peace—at least inside, within our hearts and minds, if not outside of ourselves. Many times, we cannot control the noise outside because of the many environmental stressors or taxing relationships, but we can control our own inner self. *Calm is the Water* recognizes that many people desire inner peace while also appearing to be internally conflicted with pain, venting and displacing anger on others.

Calm is the Water takes us on a journey to learn that we are in control of our inner ships and we can control and dictate how we act and react to any situation. *Calm is the Water* helps us to identify indicators that, once recognized, can initiate change in ourselves to include the crucial need for relaxation, calmness, and peaceful time devoted to ourselves, if we so choose. *Calm is the Water* provides insights and tools to begin turning down the noise and enhancing the quiet and calm that eludes us if we are not aware. *Calm is the Water* asks us to question whether we are calm, relaxed, and peaceful, and, if not, guides us to change and become exactly that, if we are ready. *Calm is the Water* assists us in identifying the noise and how to tone it down so it does not affect our health, or us, which is the main priority. *Calm is the Water* achieves this by increasing your awareness and identifying useful tools and/or insights to gently push you to the goal of inner peace. This should not be a painful experience but a process of eliminating obstacles—real or imagined— to identify a way to achieve true inner peace. We ask, "If I have problems, can I still achieve inner peace?" In addition, we ask, "If my relationships with loved ones and others are causing me undo stress, can I still cultivate inner peace?" If you are aware and realize the responsibility for your own peacefulness, *Calm is the Water* will assist you in achieving calmness and inner peace. It is all up to you. Dive in; the water is warm and calm. Be at peace

AUTHOR'S NOTE

The author, George Samuels, is an enlightened realized Spiritual Master, Guide, Teacher, Healer, Spiritual Coach, and Poet living in the San Diego area, and he is here to teach and help heal those who seek answers and to learn in order to help others. Master George has been providing light, spiritual wisdom, healing, coaching, and spiritual guidance for thousands of people throughout the USA and other countries for more than 30 years. He continues to and is currently helping and healing all who contact him seeking Light on the Path. George has written several books of poetry such as *"Audacity of Poetry," "Healing in a Word," "With Poetry in Mind," "This is Our Word," "There is Only Music Brother," "Doors to Ancient Poetical Echoes," "Lovers Should Never Quarrel,"* and *"The Song of Life."* His websites are www.spirituallifesource.com and gsamuelsbooksandart.com.

Inner Peace

(Taken from my book titled, *"Healing in a Word"*)

I am happy
I am healing
I am at peace
What is needed
Besides rest
Love is abound
My blood pressure is down
Life is unfolding
And I am growing
Life is peaceful
But comes a time
When the noise appears
Outside
I look and see
The people making the noise
Why are they here
Wow the world is at war
Noise everywhere
All the things I hold dear
Are going away
Finances are astray
My mind is thinking it is only a delay
That this is not real
It is all an illusion
That this noise is interrupting
I soar when at peace
But now am grounded
The ebb and tide is pulling
Me away
From the center
Of the pendulum
I don't want to be on the scale

Weighing in the balance
My brothers are warring
And all is not right at its place
Where we can all enjoy the best appeal
Or yield
Of our efforts
We must retain
The right balance
How is that to happen?
Of all the things in the library
No peace to be found
They say just be quiet
How so
I am looking for peace
I turn to the church
They screaming
Must be a problem
So I go home and see a glimpse
Of myself in the mirror
I see what I was looking for
Inside there is a place
Here peace resides
Behind the locked door
On the sofa
No on the mantle
In the kitchen
Oh the food is great
But the peace of food is gone
Once I ate
But then I fell asleep
Belly full
Still seeking
And realized I went to a place
That where I can be at peace
Inside
Inner peace!!!

I

BEGINNING THE JOURNEY

Can water travel uphill, transverse the landscape, and end up calm at the end of the day? Or, does it move through our veins like our minds and determine its own course? Did we wake up to all the turmoil witnessed on TV each day? Or, when we were conceived, was their peace in the waterway we travelled before appearing in the world on our own birthday?

All we can remember is life as it appeared on that first day, as we took our first breath, and opened our eyes. We hoped for peace and tranquility from our birth to now, not understanding what we sought or foresaw. We have many experiences throughout our lives as we grow to full term, whenever and however that may be. As we grow, we experience lives full of activity and we are glad for it, as life is a fast-paced series of events culminating in reaching a set of goals. Some goals are obtained by choice while others are assumed by hierarchy and are placed in our path, which is a trial by fire. At the same time we also open like a rose expressing our innate selves and what we have bought forward in the way of talents and gifts such as music, artistry, physical attributes, intelligence and/or wisdom to name a few.

We learn by doing, studying, experiencing, making mistakes, trial and error, or just trying to get it right. Some of us have problems and experiences imparted on us as if we asked for them and forgot. Sometimes, life is like white water rafting without the proper training, having skipped our swimming lessons and forgotten our life preservers at home. Some educate us by reaffirming that "I told you so;" others repeat, "you'll learn if it kills you." To these statements, we often say "whatever" and continue on experiencing what was being preached or discoursed. Otherwise we innately follow the path or the stream that has led us here and experience what it unfolds.

Therefore, with this experiential information, we go about our business discovering the things we do not know or did not realize, hoping to make it home safely. This is required in order to enjoy the little amount of time we have before finally being at peace, passing out from sheer exhaustion only to wake up again tomorrow ready, with or without the appropriate armor.

One day we will wake up and ask the question, "What happened to my peace?" as many head for the closest cave or highest mountain devoid of people. Not everyone is able to achieve a place of peace or seek peace because it may seem it is devoid of activity. Many do not believe we are supposed to be at peace—at least inside—as turmoil flows all around us like molten lava from the volcano of "what happens next?" or "what is going on around us now?" At the point when we discover there is too much white noise, we seek to figure out what is really happening. It is like a record that keeps skipping, playing the same note repeatedly. We ask ourselves why this continues and if someone will please reset the record, replace the tape, or turn off the white noise. We ask ourselves who is controlling the buttons, as issues spin in and out of control. We appreciate rest, even if only for a day. We want to be on a peaceful, perfect vacation, which we will take on some exotic island.

In Conclusion

As we begin the journey of awareness to the noise around us that has somehow integrated into ourselves, it is important to discover how to be at peace. Where there is no peace, we must become and remain calm, bringing peace into our lives and appreciating that we, too, can have access to this tremendous gift available to anyone who wants it. It does take time and inner awareness, but it can be achieved along this journey.

Next

I step across
The threshold of life
I begin my journey
Only to find I am
At the next step

What do I do
Holler or follow,
my heart
My mind leads
Me elsewhere
Why I don't know
But the chains of ignorance
Fall off me
My boat now light
Can travel far as the wind
With air under my sails
I am growing up
To hear and witness
All the noise
and the music
I cry then sigh
Laugh again, till
I realize, I am ok
And can swim the large wave
And enjoy the warm surf
For the calmness of the sea pleases me
And I get a glimpse of,
how I can be.

Next Step

We have taken the first step by asking the question, paying attention to the answer, thinking there should be one step or move we need to ascertain or discover. We realize we are at the beginning of understanding that turmoil and activity are all around and about us, but we should experience the peace, if possible and even if only for a short time. This is the beginning of what we must ask ourselves, but the sheer recognition of whether we should have a rest is at the heart of this hypothesis that we can both experience the concept and be at peace simultaneously. There are those who do not believe in the concept of peace. Others have given up on the idea, scoffing at the idea of a precious atomic particle called peace. They believe that it is only for the rich, the spiritual, and the gifted and not just for everybody. They may be right, because peace is both an internal and external choice; we can choose to experience, live, and be at peace. In order to determine if you can be at peace, you must first view and review your life from a capsule or birds-eye view regarding all the activity that has occurred and is occurring, how it is manipulating or controlling our lives—like the satellite challenger—, and whether we are at the helm. Who is operating this ship? Is it Scotty from Star Trek, the wife, family, or the boss at work? Or, is it a series of events dreamed up and put in motion as if we are stuck in a one-act play, begging the question: are we really in command? Once we have determined that, we are about to move on to the next step, which is determining where we are in the maze. How high is the white noise? Are we the principal in a one-act drama or are we just another supporting player or extra? Then, we need to determine if the noise is part of our experience—the current drama we are engaged in—or, if we are constantly writing our own improvisational screenplay and do not realize it.

In Conclusion

Why does the bird soar or the fish jump for joy out of the water? Why do people smile when no one is around? Maybe it is because they are at peace. We may not be able to ask the fish or the bird why, but we can ask ourselves. Since we have to start somewhere, we need to look at our own individual experiences and/or our current situations. Beginning to assess our own selves will be the start of our journey of self-exploration, which will set us on the path to inner peace.

II

MULTITUDE OF EXPERIENCES

How do experiences cause this phenomenon and help us to discover our inner peace, or where the white noise is coming from? Is it from the thrashing of the raging waters? Is it from the constant flow of water gushing forward or rushing all around, forcing us to swim, dive, or snorkel our way to where we need to be?

Experiences are like windows on a ship in and out of which we can look. In addition, experiences determine how we got to where we were and to where we are now. As I review my own experiences, I can see when the peace came, when it left, where it went, and how I contributed to its leaving without my awareness. Once having covered this, hopefully it will provide a roadmap re-achieving inner peace. Experiences are a string of events that make up our life, which can be either peaceful or in constant turmoil both internally and externally.

Physical Experience

This is our reality as we know it on the physical plane, and some people think that this is all there is. We can see it, feel it, touch it, brush against it, smack it, kiss it, hear it, run to it, and run from it. It is in our mirror morning, noon, and night so we can profess to know this like the back of our hand. But the question is: is this all there is for us to experience? Some of us go from event to event, situation to situation, relationship to relationship and just deal with what is presented. We flow with the harmony or the turmoil and call it action or reaction. Some people like plenty of turmoil and others want and desire calm and peace. This is personal and part of our interaction with the world that of which we are a part. This, of course, gives us the ability to control our local environment and our inner self. This gives us the opportunity to determine what we want and desire. Some people like a lot of noise and others want peace and quiet, if only to enjoy a sense of tranquility. Then there are those who not knowing the difference prefer the noise in order to feel alive and are fearful of a constant peaceful environment, physically and mentally. So if there is no noise they go about creating their own. They have forgotten there are two sides of a coin in the land of the opposites, (heads, tails; hot, cold; tall, short; etc.).

Mental Experience

When we discuss the mental experience, we get a multitude of visions. Some of these visions constitute a memory of, "I do not know," or "I vaguely remember," or "are you talking about my brain?" This is predicated on the obscure knowledge of what constitutes the brain as opposed to the mind and how they are both integrated into one organism for argument sake. However, the mind is part of the inner discovery that brings us fresh experiences, and bears fruit for us to eat and digest on a "heard but not seen" level. That is the opposite of what our parents wanted us to experience or not—namely "seen and not heard," a lovely idea, I might add.

Mental experiences come in an array of shades and colors, but they are still vivid enough for us to experience and just as powerful as those physical experiences that we feel and touch. Mental experiences make up the fullness of our mind whether in the left-brain, right brain, or the whole enchilada. We may think this is easy to discuss or explain and simple as some consider IQ numbers, but it goes deeper than that. It is as simple for us to experience as the music playing in our heads. We are still learning about the universal mind and learning how to understand its mechanics and depth. More experiences appear to be obscured to our physical vision, such as the virtual mental ocean we sometimes find ourselves immersed within. The mind is strong and can multitask, staying busy if we let it and not slowing down to relax. Like a car running all the time, we must put the gear into neutral and let it rest. The mental and physical senses work together to help us accomplish all that we do to ensure we are successful, and then it welcomes a rest period. This rest period can be momentary or longer, if required. We have a multitude of mental experiences in our mind from all we do or do not do every single day. This keeps us as busy as can be. At the same time, there are experiences that we should analyze or review. They cover a plethora of subjects that are relevant to us in our busy lives that encompass innumerable interests.

Emotional Experience

This ocean we dwell in and transverse on occasion, as we contemplate our navels, are the emotional experience that fills us with richness. This gives us depth-I-tude as we experience each other and the world at large. The emotional experience starts before one arrives at a point of wondering what all this is and why we came to be. Children exist either knowing why they are here or wondering why they are here, but they do not concern themselves with it. They are occupied with playtime and fun—if they are fortunate—so they do not have to spend their waking hours wondering what happened or did not happen. Children just enjoy their lives and are the better for it. Adults, on the other hand, experience a range or wave of emotions from relationships, likened to those in the poem below that equates relationships to ships in a sea of emotional experiences.

Relationships or Ships

Relationships have the ending word called ships
For a reason
As we ride the ocean of emotions, and
in most cases deal from an emotional basis,
that determines whether it feels good or not
Until we move to a mental level,
asking the question,
Is it good for me or,
Is it good for you?

The ride can be smooth or choppy,
depending on our willingness to tackle waves or hurricanes.
Nevertheless we take the ride.

Some of us steer our ships away from the big waves
Some of us can surf,
While others jump into the yacht and cruise.
Many are in the canoe with a hole,
bailing out the water as it fills up.
Refusing to jump into the sailboat as it breezes by
While those in the sailboat think that the wind,
should control their life.
Some play in the lake,
While others love the river of dreams
and risk takers play in the ocean,
with their oars of "do it my way,"
As the fast and fearless, motor back,
To "ride it till the wheels fall off,"
mentality.

Relationships, like ships, take us to and from ship to shore, wondering if we have landed in the right place. Or, are we in a foreign land needing to set sail or waiting for the winds to fill our sails, and the waves carry us to new lands and new relationships? This can cause us to enjoy better, the emotional nature of our interactions with others as we examine how we relate to others and how they relate to us. Beware of taking the emotional too seriously, becoming a constant wave, always in high tide, learning to understand the ebb and flow of life. Sometimes, these experiences are within our control, or unknown forces control them.

Psychic Experience

We sometimes ask ourselves, "why did this happen" or "why did this not happen," trying to figure out events beyond our control. As we move to more esoteric levels in the universe and ponder the sky, moon, and stars, we experience the internal through visions, extraordinary events, miracles, and dreams, and we meditate on the "what ifs" and "what are." This begins the psychic journey of discovering who we are on an existential and spiritual plane. Some only focus on the religious while others go to the next highest level, seeking answers to the questions, "who am I?" and "why am I who I am?" Then, we look to the stars while seeking out answers from Astrologists until we realize the answers are within us. Others seek Adepts (Spiritual Masters) who impart wisdom and information upon the unenlightened about what is not apparent. They seek answers beyond "what is for dinner?" or "who is walking the dog?" The psychic levels of experience wave their invisible hands to wake us up to the fact there is more than what we can see, hear, or feel with our regular five senses. The psychic experience, when connected to the spiritual, opens up an entire dimension to learn more about ourselves, others, our connection to the world, and the universe. This gives us access to information, insight, and wisdom into who we really are. This is essential for us to begin to discuss the idea and process of peace within our own self and the world on an exoteric level, after we investigate the esoteric. To understand the outside, one must begin to understand the inside in the same way we buy a book with a greatly designed cover and knowledge written on the pages; we do not buy the book only based on the cover.

Then, there are those experiences that we cannot easily explain. "What was that dashing by my eye?" "Did I just hear a voice?" "Wow, what a dream I had last night. I thought it was real until I woke up." "I had a vision the other day looking at the sun on the water." "The pain left and I was well again." "He picked up the 4,000-pound car to save the child, but we do not know how." These are a few of the experiences people have, and there are a multitude more that could fill up all the libraries in the world. What have you experienced? Many women say my intuition spoke to me, and I knew the answer (of course many more said I did not listen, as we smile). Additionally we deal with other experiences on a daily basis.

Psychological Experience

Psychologically, we regulate all the sensations we experience and, through minimum and maximum analyses, we determine what is in or out of order.

Many experiences require us to evaluate our pleasure and/or pain responses in order to make sense of all we know and all that affects us. We make sense of the senseless and determine what is acceptable or not acceptable. This not an easy process, but it places order in our lives and helps us to clarify what it is that we are doing and what it is we are experiencing around us. This helps us deal with those incidents and situations that we find ourselves in daily that appear to be logical or illogical, and it helps us to make sense of it as it pertains to our environment and us. The natural order of things applies to our lives just as the natural order applies to how the nature kingdom instinctively follows. We endeavor to follow and create a sense of order, maintaining that order so all appears natural and logical. We determine what is right and wrong for us, and we live by those values and gain from their principles naturally. When experiences are illogical, we question them to understand what is happening or what we are experiencing.

In Conclusion

Do we control these experiences, or do they control us? Is this all a one-act play, TV, or real life? I say, life imitates art or the reverse, which is, life is art. We all experience the art of life and make our art by painting our pictures, whether a photograph, a short story, or a full-length feature in 3D with surround sound. Others enjoy the Technicolor, but they are our experiences, and part of that is to enjoy, experience, and try to control the outcomes so they are favorable, memorable, and positive. We should be on the road to peace because war is not a place we call home. It is but a stop in traffic on the way home as we approach our off-ramp through the noise of the crowd and the beat of the street. Today, we see out-of-control road rage because patience is lost, calmness is nowhere to be found, and we cannot relax or be peaceful even as we try to practice patience. When you add up this multitude of experiences in our lives, we find lights, camera, action, and hope for positive results, such as peace and happiness. I hope that the next stop is a calm port and not raging waters!

III

RAGING WATERS

They Raged

They raged
I raged
I was quiet
They raged more
I became quieter
They raged even more
I became even more calm and quiet
They seeing it (rage) didn't work
They became quiet
And the sea of
Emotions began to
break the giant waves,
And once again the
Sea became calm
And all was at peace

Raging waters is a metaphor for what is constantly going on inside some of us, either in the mind or in the belly. Our minds sometimes churn and things that upset us cause raging waves of what to do or not to do, how to handle this and that, and where the answers are that we need at that very moment. Consider the following questions and ponder the answers:

o Are the waters around you quiet, calm, and peaceful; or, are they raging or roaring to get out?
o Do you ever find yourself relaxing, resting, calmly thinking, and strolling about, contemplating the universal?
o Are you seeking peace in your heart, expressing it to the point that it is oozing from your soul so that, when others are around you, they feel the peace simultaneously?
o Do you feel inner turmoil when you are alone after you leave work and venture home to try to rest but you cannot because the (emotional) waters inside of you are choppy and at high tide?
o Are you on a constant battleground where you work and live?

o   Do you focus on the war whether it is cold or hot, like on the TV news, which constantly displays undesirable news, justifying that this is how it is in your proverbial "neck of the woods?"

After pondering the above questions, think about what enters your mind at the same time. Do you think calm thoughts until others enter the picture, and do you then find yourself dragged into the raging waters, engulfed by their waves of controversy into which you did not intend to invite yourself? Sometimes this is where and when we begin to think to ourselves, "How did I get here and how do I get back to my center, on my boat, in my own calm waterway, to enjoy my internal peace of mind and heart?"

Some of us do not understand this because we are concerned with nonsense that continually disturbs our peace of mind. This happens every day to the point of thinking, "this is how it is" or "this is how it must be." Then, we assume that the rage—the noise, the wild waves of life—are how it is. We then think we must join in, disturbing our own peace and raging like everyone else around us so that we appear normal.

We deal with every day in a world that often affects our inner peace because many people seem to have mixed feelings or are experiencing internal pain. They vent their displaced anger on or at others that are not the source of their anger. Other people did not cause the problems in you, and often people do not understand why they are experiencing the vented anger or pain you are expressing because you do not know how to release it, let it go, and not let it affect those who are not involved. I am certain you have heard the phrase, "If they are not happy then no one around them will be either."

When we meet others who appear to be at peace and calm, we think they are abnormal, not realizing they are actually the normal ones. We explain to them that they are out of touch. A woman once told me that something was wrong with me because I did not like to argue on a daily basis. She explained to me that life was about turmoil, then making up–that was her definition of relationships. And if I did not get with the program, she was out. She finally left, upset and raging to her delight. I smiled because we were both happy at the outcome. Another time I met a woman who cursed me one day because she stated I was too happy, and she could not stand it. I smiled and understood. Over the years when I see her, she looks at me as if I am the problem, even though we are just passing each other on the street.

Once I was asked, "how could you meditate in a stadium at a football game?" I explained that it was I at the game with everyone else, so I am free to do what I like without being distracted. This is because inner peace is within you. You can maintain it anytime you choose. The agitation, the turmoil, the waves of emotion such as anger, depression, hate, and sadness are only with you shortly, and you have the innate ability to turn it on or off at any time you choose. Monks meditate to be calm, spiritual, and able to relax, trying not to get overexcited about every little detail. Children can be quite emotional when they are young because, most times, they are experiencing life like the proverbial wave in the ocean: one day is calm and the next day involves changes like an emotional roller coaster. Many people feel and speak of their lack of control, so they just do or act hoping someone will come along and calm them down. I have had friends who were fortunate because they are or have a wife that has calmed them down. So, instead of expressing overt anger, they are now much more calm and peaceful.

What do you do when you find yourself out of control or when the emotions you feel do not subside? Do you take a rest, center yourself, use a code word, or get a massage to help you relax? Do you have someone to rescue you or a magic pill? Are you constantly working on training yourself to avoid becoming overexcited? Are you in the habit of making excuses, blaming someone else? Are there times you were calming others down instead of exciting them, or do you encourage them to be stimulated because you need some excitement in your life? Ponder these questions above and jot down your responses. They provide little clues to assist you when you ponder the next questions.

_____

_____

_____

_____

_____

_____

Do you want to be at peace and happy but others won't let you? Or, are you unable to make the appropriate decisions advocating for your own peace of mind and existence? Many say the rage is outside, and they are just following the crowd. Others think life is about expecting change so it will facilitate the noise we hear, knowing it will eventually change.

The Light of the day is upon us, and we are learning to accept those things we cannot change. However, when it was first explained, we discussed the external. We have full control over our own self, and we can begin to let go and release all the negative volatile ideas, relax and be happy inside no matter what is happening outside. Peace is a state of mind and heart. When we experience so many issues and situations, we have to protect ourselves from worry, tension, stress, and the possibility of losing control. We do not realize we can stay detached from all the noises and waves coming at us from all directions. How can we do this? We have to look at our current situation, and any or all problems we are currently experiencing. Some people only know one speed: rage or not to rage.

Recently a man was driving home with his wife and young infants when another young man driving another car accidently cut him off while trying to make a left hand turn. Instead of letting the young man go on his way, the man in the car with his family flew into a rage and chased the young man down with his car, a young man who was twenty years his junior and 60 pounds lighter. After running the young man off the road, he jumped out of his car, opened the door of the young man's car, and grabbed him, proceeding to beat the teenager senseless while his wife and babies watched. Then, he wondered why he was in court and had to pay for the young man's medical expenses. When asked why he left his family and flew into an uncontrollable rage, he stated that he only thought about attacking the young man because he inadvertently cut him off and the young man was making an illegal turn. He wanted to teach him a lesson. He completely forgot about his wife and babies left in the car. His rage took over and he did not care about anything else, including his family.

In Conclusion

This type of inner rage or outrage is out of control. Some of us rage to a lesser degree, but it still requires us to stop ourselves from becoming angry with little, or so-called, big things. Out-of-control anger can cause us to rage. That is why the old adage goes, "be slow to anger," teaching us not to get angry or become out of control so quickly that we do not even think about what we are doing or whether it is even worth it. Sometimes the rage is inside, but we must let it go safely and focus on being calm, instead. Like a fire, one should pour water on it and allow it to dissipate as it turns into steam or hot air, avoiding harm to us or anyone else. We sometimes experience things or events that cause us to become upset, but we can control this by remaining calm. Sometimes in relationships, we are told to sleep off our anger in order to keep it under control or to cool down. We laugh when we hear some people need anger management, but that is for those of us who cannot control our emotions and need to seek outside assistance. This is a good idea if you cannot do it on your own. The word we should keep in our minds and hearts, besides love, is calm; use it often, especially those who carry deadly weapons and think it is acceptable to lose control.

IV

PROBLEMS VERSUS SOLUTIONS

I wandered down the avenue thinking to myself how I was going to solve the situation at work where certain colleagues were trying to generate a rift between my boss and myself. Every day they complained about every little thing, and I was worrying that my boss was listening to them, even thinking I might lose my job. Every day I spent time after work thinking what I could do. Finally, I went to my boss and complained about my co-workers watching every little thing I did or did not do. Shocked, he said he had not paid the co-workers any attention; he wondered what my problem was and whether he needed to look into the situation. I then realized I was worrying about nothing and there was no issue with my boss—save for my panicking for no reason. I then decided to ignore whatever my co-workers were engaged in and I focused on my work.

This is a case in point for why, sometimes, worrying about nothing can create problems. Problems are divided into two categories: real and imagined. Real problems are those that have a cause and effect, and we must solve those problems so they will go away. Problems that are imagined or fantasy-based are problems created by illusions that we assume are real, but after thorough investigation, we realize they may be imaginary. After investigation, they can be dismissed, and, upon doing so, they stop being a problem. Some people perpetuate these imaginary problems, making us believe there is a real problem. Alternatively, they escalate a small situation into a big problem. This happens until we realize they are creating something from nothing. Then, we learn and understand that imaginary problems have no effect on us. It is important to understand the distinction between the two because stressful situations sometimes make us believe we have problems, whether they are real or not. This can cause us to act out in a way that makes us believe the problems are real and active until we approach the problems with a view of how to solve them. If not solved, the problems will continue to escalate until they solve themselves, if possible, or disappear from where they came (if illusionary). Problems give us opportunities to create solutions so that we can successfully stop worrying and live a problem-free life. Small problems can sometimes be easily solved or dismissed. Alternatively, larger problems are more difficult to solve because we observe whether we can solve it on our own. Problems need to be solved, and we should spend our time creating or seeking solutions and not dwelling on the problems themselves, churning over them until we worry endlessly. This often creates other problems or makes small problems grow larger.

Most Problems are Temporary

The most important thing to remember is that most problems are temporary, they will pass, and we will solve them eventually. A problem should not define your life. You are your life, and a problem is just a temporary, minor aspect of your total life experience. All problems should be relegated and dealt with, even if it is an emergency. While solving your problems, stay centered in your life to be and remain calm and collected. This way, you can see the rest of what is transpiring in your life and allocate the appropriate amount of attention or focus. Even in a boat in the middle of the ocean, one has to remain balanced through a momentary storm so huge waves will not turn the boat over. Like the sea, we should be centered and calm enough to see what we need to do to get to dry land through the storm. We can relish in how we handled the situation, and we can now move on calmly and at peace with the knowledge that we solved the problem. This may sound simple, but as complex as we are in our multifaceted lives, we can stay and be centered and calm enough to ride out any temporary waves. This is accomplished by focusing on the solution and knowing that, inside, it is important to be calm and at peace no matter what. We all have analytical skills that give us the ability to solve problems, and, if we do not, we seek advice from trusted sources that will not take advantage of our situation or vulnerability. They can provide solid, unbiased advice to help us solve any problem we feel we cannot solve ourselves. Even then, we should remain calm and centered enough to see or realize the solution. We can help ourselves, and we can always find appropriate assistance to help us. This should give us a calming effect to trust ourselves and trust that we can solve any problem presented to us. This will help us overcome any current obstacles or those we may encounter in the future.

In Conclusion

We must try to focus not on the problem but on the solution, and then we will not worry as much. A hungry person does not care, which came first, the chicken or the egg; they just want to eat to erase the empty feeling in their belly. If your mind is focused on what is wrong with you, then you will never think about what is right, which might be just in front of you. Why is it that we sometimes panic first then think about what we can do? Sometimes we get upset and lose control only to find out that we have overreacted. Most do not need to be slapped back from the brink of having lost it all only to find out we can calmly solve the problem or situation ourselves. The most important thing to reinforce is to not immediately panic.

Like a ladder, we must climb over all our problems and obstacles to find the best solutions. Remember to focus on the solution and, at the same time, remain calm. As we solve problems, we learn from them in order not to repeat them. It will also serve to assist others when they have similar problems and are in search of solutions. Once a problem is determined, then solved, focus on the present and future and not on the past. Do not let problems be or become an obstacle. Later, ponder what we have learned or gained from the experience and then move forward.

V

OBSTACLES

Obstacles are problems that appear to be perceived as real or imaginary that we think are in our way. Sometimes, we feel they are blocking us from solving our problems, but, like problems, we can remove and solve them. At first, when we see a tree across the road blocking us from going forward, we think it is a major obstacle. As soon as the tree is removed, we realize the obstacle is no more and is now gone from our path. Sometimes, we think a problem is insurmountable and an obstacle to any solution. However, we have to know that obstacles are just a perception, whether real or not, that can be removed from our minds or from our path to understand there is a solution to any problem we may be experiencing.

Obstacles are like a stone in the road that can be pushed aside and out of our way or dissolved because it is not a permanent reality. It is just an illusion that was once recognized, and it will dissipate from whence it came. Some people say the obstacle is too large, but there is no obstacle larger than the universe or larger than your mind. Thus, it can be scaled or circumvented around to accomplish what is needed. Again, when a tree falls on the road, the obstacle is removed soon enough to allow the traffic to continue to flow. With a ladder, we climb up and over anything in our way, but there are perceptions that cause us to think we cannot do something we can. Some of these things create illusions that cause some problems to seem real or huge. So, we need to know they are not real. Some problems are just waves in an ocean, and they will go out with the tide if we release them.

Some of these are as follows:

- Stress
- Worry
- Negativity
- Impatience
- Old wounds (emotional)
- Outside Influences and Disturbances
- Environmental factors
- Debts

Which of these indicators are real or imaginary? Many people suffer from the above criteria but do not understand these appear to be obstacles preventing you from being calm, centered, and at peace with their own self. If you ask, many people will say these are all real, but the truth is, only two of these are actually real. Can you guess which ones? It is the debts and environmental factors. The other indicators are not real obstacles; they are imaginary, even though they appear to some as real. These indicators can be dismissed or dissipated like rain, as soon as you realize that you can release them. So what does that mean? It means that, if you have a problem, do not worry, do not stress, do not think negative thoughts, and do not let outside disturbances affect you or stop you from solving your problems or overcoming any obstacles you might encounter. In addition, by not allowing any of these perceived or real obstacles to affect you, one can then remain calm, centered, and at peace in the wake of dealing with problems.

Imaginary Problems

Often, we have to deal with real problems, outside influences, other people's problems, drama, and paranoia. However, we seldom discuss our own paranoid or imaginary thoughts nor do we discuss the things we allow to infiltrate our minds that are not real but still affect us. Some of these imaginary problems or thoughts come from life as we deal with what imitates art, but many imitate the art of living and dealing with what is presently happening or has happened in our local environment. Life then causes us focus on what it is and how we react to real or perceived problems. We become stressed, and we then find ourselves pre-maturely reacting to perceived real or not so real triggers. This disturbs our inner peace because we are essentially on edge and sensitized to respond to any real or imaginary environmental stimuli. Subsequently, we find ourselves reacting or overreacting without completely investigating the situation before we react or overreact. This type of disturbance upsets us internally, we react inwardly, and it disturbs our own inner peace. We have to let go of this paranoia in order to restore that inner peace and not react to stimuli that appear to rock our boat and disturb our calm.

In Conclusion

There are real problems that we deal with every day and we must take care of them, so we do not negate them, but we must distinguish between the real and the imagined problems. This is important because sometimes people take a minor problem and re-imagine it as a giant problem. This then causes us to overreact to the point that our minor problem becomes larger than it is or we panic, worry, or become upset, only to find out it was minor or imagined. When we are faced with real problems, we must still remain calm and handle them by finding the solution. With imaginary problems, we must be able to sense whether a problem is real, whether it is minor or major, and whether it is our problem so we can relax and remain calm.

As we distinguish whether problems are real or imagined, we should remain centered, calm, solve all problems, and move all obstacles from our way. This requires us to think about the problem or obstacle and whether "this, too, shall pass." If it is temporary it will pass. At the same time, one should not volunteer to take on other people's problems and make them their own. We should investigate the cause calmly when confronted with a problem. Many times, that will be an indication whether the problem is real or imagined and what the possible solution might be. Always, imagine the obstacle is gone from your path instead of it blocking the way. Visualize the solution.

VI

SUN AND RAIN EXPLAINS

I Question

I question
Does the sun warm as it burns
Does the rain grow flowers
As it drowns the land
Can you separate the
Rain from the hurricane
Does warm rain
Bring Mayflowers
Is the sun a reflection of
the moon or visa versa
Can I learn from
The sun and moon everyday
Does the peace turn to warm
As the floods turn to water the lawn
As does peace come after the storm
Is a baby at peace
While the parents worry
Much more than we see
Without the sun and rain,
To explain

Can we actually,
Understand the difference
Between war and peace
Or does the five elements
(water, fire, earth, metal, air)
Reveal all we need to be
For when we are in turmoil
all we can hope for
Is a little peace.

When the sun shines, many people feel great, happy, and tranquil; then, when it rains, they, all of a sudden, change their demeanor and then feel sad, upset, and depressed. This can cause that up-down feeling, like the waves in the ocean. As we see there are calm waters with little or no waves, we realize that it is the nature, and we should address the sun and rain in the same way and we should not be moved inwardly because of a change in the weather; we know it is only temporary, it will change, and pass. Our inner position should be to stay centered, calm and peaceful. This will then allow us to focus on the positive idea that both the sun and rain are special for us and help us to grow our food, feed us energy and keep us alive and healthy. Now, that is something to smile about and to be at peace with at the same time. Then we can spend more time focusing on oneself instead of what is happening outside and all over the country–things that will pass in a day's time.

It rains on everyone, so we should not judge others but only judge our self. The sun shines not only in the sky but also in our hearts if we let it. It should not be raining in your heart; feel the power of the sun. Let it shine and express all the love within your heart for you first, and then for others in your heart. If there are any grudges, hurt, or anger, let them go. They do not belong in your heart. Whatever you have in your heart that you do not like or want or is not representative of you—positive and loving—, then release it so you can be you. This places you on the road to inner peace because our hearts, when full of love, can see the happy sun shining and the sea will calm down as we float to the gentle peaceful shores within.

In Conclusion

The weather is representative of our lives and the situations we deal with on a daily basis. Sometimes it is cold, sometimes warm, and sometimes too hot. When it rains, it pours; other times, it snows. But, we learn to shovel it out of the way and move forward.

Let us try to look out the window and see the beauty of the sun, the rain, the flowers, the peace, and the tranquility before the storm and after the sun goes up and down. Remember that tomorrow brings a new day for us to appreciate ourselves and be at peace inside as we surround ourselves with love!

VII

FOCUS ON YOU

Why focus on you? Why focus on the outside actions and activities on the other side? For example, some focus on looking outside the window more than looking in the mirror. Often, we focus on what is going on around us like the car, bills, friends, family, work, etc. We are also drawn into other people's lives via the television and the Internet. Since many people are being wasting time on social media, we must also understand this. Social media are becoming intrusive and interconnected with our everyday activities, as if it were an extension of our physical selves. We must learn and/or turn in to our center to realize all outside is exactly that, and inside, in the center, is where we need to pay attention. This way, we can relax and not let all that is going on outside affect our inner center and disturb our inner calm or peace. Difficult as it may seem, we can be undisturbed by all the noise outside and around us. Develop the ability to stay centered and calm, and endeavor to be at peace no matter what is being ruffled, twisted, and pulled in chaotic directions, like what is exhibited in the news.

Yes, being calm and at peace is an art that we can nurture, attained by staying centered, calm, and at peace, even if we are dealing with worldly, personal problems and difficult situations. We live in a time where there are unjust wars, but even though we are in shock and against this, we can remain calm and centered with the hope that it will be discontinued. However, we do not have to have war at home or within ourselves. This inner space within should be the place of the true home and peace, even if we live in a house where there are factors trying to pull us off-center. Imagine you are at peace inside, and then there will be peace in the home.

Arguments do not start themselves and arguments do not continue by themselves. When you are at peace, you exude an aura of peace, and those who sense this and want to disturb that will not succeed if you do not allow them; stick to the center of who you are.

We stand in waves of water, but the riptides that come and go in life do not draw us out if we do not allow them. We can remain calm and wait for everything to settle so we are able to ride the tide of small waves. That is the compromise we are make within ourselves to remain at peace, similar to calm water spreading across the sea, relaxing its flow and becoming ever so calmer.

In Conclusion

Who comes first in your life, you or everyone else? Do you take care of you or others first? Remember that on a boat or plane, the captain, always tells you to put on your oxygen mask or life preserver first, then anyone else's, including loved ones. This is because you have to make sure you are all right first. Therefore, the lesson here is that we must focus on us, and we must remember that we know peace and it knows us, so we can be calm and at peace if we focus on being centered. The same goes with when we are busy in a world full of tasks and other duties. As we deal with all that is going on around us, we can calmly view what we need to do or choose to deal with in our environment. Remember when we stand in the pool as the water surrounds us, it only moves when we move and are still when we become still.

VIII

HARMONIZING YOU AND YOUR ENVIRONMENT

As we focus and begin to know where we are, then we can better interact within our local environment by being in harmony and handling situations from a perspective that enables us to see all sides. Then, we can determine how we will deal with the waves that pass by us, whether the tide is going out or coming in. Using this as a metaphor for disturbances, interactions, and difficult situations that we deal with on a daily basis helps us to understand our obstacles.

When we swim with the tide, we avoid the riptides and, if caught in a riptide, we are taught to go with it, calmly ride it out, turn at the right time, and swim back to land. This is how we survive difficulties and become a success of our own destiny and the captain of our own fate. Yes, we are in control, even when it seems we are not. We can be at peace and we can be calm no matter what is going on around us.

How do we do this? We begin to move from that calm, peaceful center and harmonize ourselves in a way that allows us to move and flow with what is happening around us. We begin to choose what we deal with, what we avoid, and how we handle the noise and the daily drama that tries to summon us to trivial battles. These battles sometimes have nothing to do with us except that they present unnecessary excitement and entertainment. Even when situations and events appear serious today, we react only to find out tomorrow it was all meaningless and just creating a loud noise. Just like the person who kicks the can down the road. As we are calm and centered, we start to understand what is relevant to deal with and what drama to stay away from, and we begin to think what disharmonizes us. We then can quickly get back to our centered attention on being at peace within, as we are not as easily drawn into other people's noise and drama.

If you step into the ocean and you see the waves are too big to handle, you are supposed to know to step out of the ocean, back onto dry land, and wait for calmer seas and waves. As we are at peace, we will naturally harmonize all who are around us. Therefore, when people come around us they will sense this and also become calm, or have a negative reaction to the harmony they need to seek in their own lives. Have you ever had friends or family come over to your home and say, "Wow, I feel at peace while I am in your home and environment?" That is you expressing your harmony; your inner peace that seeps out, affecting your local outward environment. That is why many people, when reaching home after a long day, first say upon entering their own homes, "They are now at peace." This is true, and you can take that peace with you throughout your day; but you have to be careful that you stay centered and calm, not reacting to whatever is happening on your way to and from home. The good news is that you can express this inner calm and peace, and it will reach out to others who can sense this and may benefit from it, but only if they realize they also can duplicate the same inner peace within their own self.

In Conclusion

This sounds easy, and it is, but it takes attention and awareness to know when you are centered, when you are off-centered, when you are not calm, or when you are not letting the outside noise affect your inner calmness. So, how do we achieve this without staying home in our bed under the covers, blocking out the public, turning off the cable, the Internet, and the social media? Great question, yes, but there is not an easy answer. As we become more adept at staying calm and out of the drama, we have to begin pushing the water out that is coming into the boat. If the boat has a hole in it, we must plug it up and start to turn away from the drama or solve the immediate disrupting situation to return to a sense of tranquility. As we become more tranquil, we see the waves coming and know what to avoid, how to react, or what to stay away from and avoid. Even as we deal with the outside world, we will whisper to our inner self the word, "calm." We will recognize the general noise that is just noise and realize there is no need to deal with it. This sense of calm and tranquility will permeate our minds and hearts, and we will want to share it with our local environments. In addition, we will not react to those trying to push our so-called proverbial buttons. In order to harmonize ourselves, we need to distinguish what type of noise we are dealing with. It is a good exercise to say to ourselves when we are becoming tense and need to become unfettered to quietly say "I am calm and centered" three times, then relax. Then think to quietly, "I am at peace."

IX

Turning Away from the Noise

External and Physical Noise

Yes, we have to turn away from all the noises we hear and we are inundated with on a daily basis. Hour by hour, we hear and experience many types of noises such as,

- garbage trucks
- fire engines
- police cars
- helicopters
- taxicabs
- ambulances
- phones ringing

Add to that the noise created by the multitude of buses, trucks, and cars. There is noise from the people hollering, from the arguments that do not include us, from work related noise, from the daily activities of friends and families, from TV dramas like the news, from divisive politics, from daily living, and from all the stuff one deals with each and every hour of our day. We also create a lot of noise with all of the mechanized toys and tools we use on a daily basis. This includes the clanging in the house with our fixing, updating, and changing of this and that to satisfy our momentary whims.

Did you ever go to lunch by yourself and listen to the decibel levels or listen to the family buffet—the noise from the pots, pans, and dishes dropping to the beat of broken china. Jet planes have their own decibel levels, especially if they are military planes. Everyone is distracted by sounds, which are an example of the outside noises we experience on a daily basis. Some of these external noises are upsetting to our internal peace and equilibrium, but we deal with it and allow the varied noises to disturb our inner peace and stability. It does not stop there. Smells and the things we visualize that interact with our senses or sensibility create noise.

Internal and Mental Noise

Internally, we have noises that we also experience, from our own heartbeat to the internal sounds of air and gas to our mental interactions that are personal to one's own self. Mental noise can include the distractions that we entertain when we think about our plans, activities, or those external distractions that we contemplate repeatedly, sometimes called worry, which involve concerns about our daily lives, personal plans, and relationships. We have complex brains and minds and we can mentally consider either what is on the pinhead of a needle or what is happening in the external universe.

We spend endless hours concerned about our health and wellbeing, and that includes our prosperity. At the same time, we spend countless hours contemplating "what if" scenarios about almost everything we do or do not do, should or should not do. Mentally, it takes a toll on our inner peace because sometimes we are not in total control of the outcomes. We have to debate inwardly different types of beginning-, middle-, or end-game scenarios or one-act plays to fill our minds to stop overthinking, worrying ourselves, and creating endless amounts of stress that impact our lives. In addition, it affects our health and wellbeing without anyone advising us to relax and stop the worrying in order to get back to our inner state of peace and centeredness. It is not so easy to turn off the noise outside, unless we move to the mountaintop or the cave, just as it is not so simple to turn off the inner mental noise we create by just saying "shut up" to oneself. Although, those who are adept can shut off the noise, become centered, and be at peace, at least for a moment, until it is broken by some internal or external distraction.

It is important, if not imperative, to be able to learn how to ignore and turn away from the noise to begin to attain inner peace. It is achievable at some perceptible level. Some say they cannot do it; not because they cannot but because they have not even tried or they have given up. They think the external noises are the same as the internal noises and that it is all normal. It is true that you cannot alleviate the noise until you have reached a level of inner peace. First, you must understand that there are noises coming from different places, some you cannot control, such as external noises, and some you can control, such as internal or mental noises.

The first thing one must know is that there is such a state as inner peace and it is achievable at some rudimentary and adept level, if you elect to begin the journey, strive, and continue until you reach the level of inner peace. For example, many people say they cannot meditate, or it is impossible to be quiet, even for a moment. It is not the truth. One has to begin by controlling the effect the outer noises have on our self, such as not being upset or overly disturbed when one hears loud, overbearing noises that are external and cannot be turned off. In addition, one has to begin to search within and find a place of relaxation. We must begin to calm our surging emotional reactions to every little distraction or disturbance. For example, some people get internally upset at every little disturbance, even though the noise is external or affecting something personal. We have used the phrases "slow to anger" and "stay calm through adversity." These are small indications that one should stay calm under most or all circumstances.

Noise of the Fight

Fighting the noise is obvious, but fighting is a subject one must discuss to understand aggressive noise. Fighting is noisy, but more aggressive and more invasive. Many people have been in fights initiated by others such as bullies, enemies, competitors, etc. Fighting makes a loud noise before, during, and after the fight. Fighting is all about noise; not only about the outer, external noises but also about the internal noises, rumblings, unsettledness, and lack of inner peace. Many people want to fight, go to war, or start trouble to help express the inner noise of the raging waters inside. Where does this noise come from? It can come from the heart, mind, and stomach, full of a sea of unbridled emotions and simple triggers that are generated from the ego or a false sense of pride. It is difficult for some not to respond to these undercurrents before they grow and lose control, instead of responding in a peaceful manner. Some people have been taught to react and respond with a loud noise when dealing with others, as they have observed others responding in a similar manner. This also can include witnessing violence, hearing loud noises, and seeing altercations within their local environments.

One day, I was walking up the street when I came across several of friends in my neighborhood. Upon greeting each other, we exchanged words, and they went on about their business. After the rest of the group left, one of the men who was with his girlfriend turned to me and explained that we was going to beat me up. I remained calm within, as I assessed the situation first. After a couple of moments, I decided I had a choice: I could either fight and beat him up, or I could choose to help him by stating that it was in his best interest to delay the fight until he was alone. He questioned why he would or should delay the fight. I explained that if he lost the fight to me, his girlfriend would witness him getting beat up, and she would have little respect for him and leave him, as he was the one that initiated the altercation. After a couple of minutes and turning to his girlfriend, he agreed that he had better walk away so he would not be embarrassed in front of his girlfriend. Now, I could have taken his challenge. I knew he had little chance of winning, but I realized why I should not disturb my inner peace for someone seeking trouble through his or her noise to prove a point; there is no need. Once he made his decision, I turned and smiled as he calmed down and left, smiling with his lovely girlfriend.

Many people feel they must be and act tough, use violence, or loud noises to defending themselves, starting fights to prove how tough they are. Others feel they must become as loud as possible and respond in a similar manner to prove they can be just as loud, obtrusive, or tough. The noise can get louder as one feeds into it, like oxygen to a fire and a leak to a flood. One does not realize it is a reflection of the state of our inner self, even though it is not our inner self. We say it takes two to start a fight or to tango, but it also takes one to stop a fight or turn down the noise. Some people think it is because we must represent that we are warriors, but there is a difference between a warrior and a fighter, who fights because they can. The truth is that a true warrior knows when to fight, how to control himself, whom to fight, when not to fight, and when, most importantly, to put the sword down, seeking only peace and tranquility.

When you meet the type of person who tries to draw you into their noise, you must remember it is their noise, not your own. Sometimes, it is easy for others to try and provoke us by saying things they hope will increase the volume of the noise, such as insults, belittlement, or idle threats that encourage us to join in. You have the ability to ignore and avoid this kind of noise when you realize you cannot be turned that easily because, internally, you are at peace. Yes, you could respond to the noise, but choosing not to and maintaining your inner peace and centeredness, most times, will cause the noise to lower. This thereby diminishes the raging tide of the person making the noise, which often comes from inner urgings and seeking or creating trouble where there is none. The fight is not within you but within the initiators own inner self, as they seek opponents or adversaries onto whom they can project their noise. You must listen to your own inner self, know that you are not the problem or the instigator, and be true to your own self (meaning be honest to yourself, you are in charge of yourself). It is easy to be drawn in, but it is just as easy to stay centered within and to not step out of your own circle.

When those making loud noises challenge us, we must choose to walk away or avoid it when we sense they are looking to instigate a fight or altercation in order to satisfy their need to express or project their noise on unsuspecting people. Again, it is easy to be drawn in, but it is just as easy to stay centered within and to not step out of your own inner circle. Once, when I was riding the train, there were two men talking amongst themselves. All of a sudden, a man sitting next to them began shouting expletives at them and threatening violence by calling them hostile names. The two men turned to deal with the man seeking to start trouble, but one of the men stated, "Oh, he is looking for trouble. Ignore him; we are having a good day. Let's not get drawn into his nonsense and mess up our day," as the two men exited the train. The man who tried to begin an altercation just watched and decided to remain quiet for the remainder of his time on the train. I was proud that these two men saw through the noise and decided not to be drawn in, staying centered and at peace and ignoring the noise around them. When confronted, it is possible to ignore, walk away, or not entertain the noise being presented, especially that which has nothing to do with you.

In Conclusion

As you begin to understand the difference between noise and peace, it will quell your thirst for peace. You will be able to ignore idle noise that has nothing to do with you. Fighting, win or lose, is just loud noise, which is not your goal. Do not think that because you did not respond, you are a coward; instead, realize that you are smart and wise because you will not be provoked to prove how tough you are, proving how calm and peaceful you are. You will show how you do not respond to external noise. Obey yourself and you will not let others manipulate you into steering your proverbial boat into their riptide of unsettled raging waters that exist within them. When you tone down the rhetoric and smile within, you will see the noise dissipate as you walk away toward the peace within you. A wise man has nothing to prove to you. Whether you fight with the noise or not, it is up to you; only you can determine whether your inner peaceful self resonates with you or whether some other person's noise does, as they fight within, trying to find others to join in their noise. Many with less understanding and little inner peace seek to have allies when making loud noises, and they need help to create loud noises. You can join them; or, you can remember that water seeks its own levels and so does noise. Remember that only you can turn up or down the noise to become quiet and remain peaceful.

X

MUSIC IS ALSO
AN ANSWER

Calmness and centeredness go hand in hand, and they require us to relax and quiet our own self while we are dealing with everything from external disturbances to internal actions; these things exist within as we handle all that is required on a daily basis. Another method many use to gain inner peace is meditation, prayer, chanting, and listening to relaxing music. Others take moments to be quiet or have rest so that, both internally and externally, they can relax, be calm, center themselves, and experience inner peace. These techniques will help the individual to relax if disturbed or calm down and center oneself to attain peace in stressful situations. These techniques are very effective in helping one to control their emotions, release and control their stress, and improve their health and wellbeing. This sounds easy to some and difficult to others, but it is achievable if one aspires to reach and cultivate a level of inner peace. Some people need assistance or advice from one who has walked the path or has achieved inner peace within their own lives. Therefore, if needed, one should seek those who can be the difference between success and failure.

Do not give up what is and what could be a benefit to your own life in helping you to rise above the noise that tries to drown out your essence or inner music, while it plays a song of peace. It is an everyday achievement; persevere in order to reap the reward and enjoy the quietness and peace that is yours! Study meditation; listen to calming music that helps you to relax. Being calm slows incessant thinking, melts anxiety, and dissipates anger. Music comes in many varieties, and it will assist you when you need to relax and be calm; whatever makes you happy. Music has been used as a healing solution for many generations. There is inner music, but we have to relax and be at peace to hear it; calmly listen until you hear it. Our hearts seek to be quiet and they wish that we would listen so we could hear what was inside; in order to do that, we must become very quiet and listen.

In Conclusion

I know it is easy to say and harder to accomplish, but it is possible. How, you ask? One must develop a state of calm, even though some situations challenge our calmness. One must learn to develop a level of centeredness, or being heart-centered. This is so that, no matter what is happening now, we do not "fly off the handle" or lose control within our own being. We may have to react outside, but as we learn to stay calm, our responses will remain so, as well.

Music is known to reduce tension, anxiety and stress after being listened to for a short period. Music has a calming effect. If you cannot calm yourself, try listening to music to assist you. Choose a few songs that make you relax, feel calm, and experience peacefulness. Play them when you feel the need.

XI

TECHNIQUES TO BEGIN THE PROCESS OF CREATING INNER PEACE

Make Changes in Your Life Checklist

This checklist is only intended to create awareness. The questions or statements below are questions we do not face or ask ourselves, but they are vital to address as we move forward to a place of inner peace. It is required that we know certain answers and that we have self-examined ourselves to facilitate our understanding of external and internal factors that affect us most. The questions are divided into several categories to assist you in understanding the insight that may be required to clear any doubt or obstacles, even those we may not have considered. For example, I used to live in a house on a street where, every morning, garbage trucks would make an enormous amount of noise because their garage was only one block away. At the same time, several neighbors had motorcycles and, every day, they would tune and rev up their bikes when I was trying to sleep before going to work. The incessant noise was so overwhelming on a daily basis that, eventually, I moved to a neighborhood that was much quieter. Ask yourself these questions or ponder these statements below. They might add insight, bring up new questions, or provide answers. At the end of the chapter, there is space for you to write down your answers or observations.

Noise

1. What noises disturb you?
2. Look for where the noise is coming from, externally.
3. Determine what types of noise bother you.
4. Determine if the noise is at home, inside, or outside. Is the noise at work, in the general area, or the community?
5. Look to see who is causing the noise. Is it environmental, personal or are people causing it?
6. Which noises are beyond your control, and which are within your control?
7. Determine if you are the noise creator or a major contributor to the noise.

Change

8. Determine if you can change anything or nothing.
9. Look at yourself, as if in the mirror, and determine if you are creating inner noise from overthinking, worrying, overstressing, or talking in your head to the point that it causes stress or fatigue.
10. Can you envision yourself calm, at peace, and happy either now or in the future?

Challenge

11. Determine if you are thinking or feeling paranoid, real, or illusionary.
12. Determine the challenges you perceive to be keeping you from being relaxed, calm, centered, and peaceful.
13. Are there overwhelming problems you are dealing with that are disturbing your calm, centeredness, and inner peace?
14. Do you rest your mind?
15. Is your mind running on its own?
16. Has anger taken over?
17. Have you given up on being peaceful?
18. Are you holding grudges from the past against others?
19. Are you depressed because things do not always go your way?
20. Are you blaming others for you not being happy or peaceful?
21. Are there wars within that you need to solve first?
22. Do you believe you can be at peace?
23. Are you ready to be more relaxed, and to begin cultivating peace within your life?

Outside Influences

24. Determine if others are causing you to be distressed, disturbed, or feel off-centered.
25. Does work leave you exhausted and stressed every day?
26. Do you take vacation? If yes, how many times per year?
27. Is someone preventing you from becoming peaceful?

28. Are you allowed to relax and be calm at home, or is it a stressful environment where you have to leave to relax and be at peace?
29. Can you relax when you come home after a busy day?
30. Are you mad at past situations?
31. Do you have displaced anger?

Inside Influences

32. Determine when you are most stressed, calm, overwhelmed, at peace, fearful, and relaxed.
33. Determine how you are sabotaging your own calm, relaxation, and peace of mind.
34. When, during your day, do you fell most stressed?
35. Are you in charge of you and your life?
36. Are you too stubborn to change?
37. Do you deserve to be happy and at peace?
38. What is in your heart and mind?
39. Are you willing to let go of old news?
40. Are you sleeping well?
41. Are you going to bed and sleeping properly?
42. Are you experiencing fears about starting on the path to peace?
43. Are you hateful or loving?

The Practice

44. Are you ready to begin the day or do you need to think about it?
45. Determine when you can spend time during your day relaxing, remaining calm, and being at peace.
46. Do you know how to meditate or do you need to learn?
47. Can you meditate? If so, when do you practice during your busy day?
48. Are you currently practicing meditation?
49. Are you resting properly in the evening or napping during the day?
50. When do you take time for you during your day, week, or month?
51. Are you ignoring yourself in your busy life, or are you paying attention to only others?

52. Do you pray for peace?
53. Are you ready to make changes in your life to attain inner peace or find the path to peace?
54. Do you have a special room where you can be at peace at home?
55. Do you try to relax and stay centered everyday no matter what?
56. Do you feel at peace inside yourself?
57. Can you allow yourself to be happy and peaceful?
58. Are you willing to begin to work to bring more calm, relaxation, and peace to your life?
59. What tools are you currently using to stay relaxed, calm, centered, and to be at peace within and throughout, no matter the circumstances?
60. Have you reached a certain level of calm and inner peace on your own? If so, do you want to attain an even more centered and deeper inner peace?
61. Are you currently practicing any forms, such as yoga, or internal kung fu, such as t'ai chi ch'uan, or qigong, that are bringing you to a place of inner peace?

In Conclusion

The above indicators will cause you to think and assess where you are as well as what may be helping you to gain inner peace. In addition, they may help you to identify what is pulling you away from your inner center, causing you undue stress and tension, and disturbing your calm and inner peace. Sometimes, we struggle to figure out what is bothering us while dealing with busy life. We do not take a moment to sit down or ask about all that is going on, keeping us over active and unable to relax completely, even when we are supposed to or when we are at home. After reviewing the above criteria, your mind will be opened to introspect and your inner and outer awareness will increase; then, we can use these to evaluate what changes need to be instituted as we see fit. Some indicators will resonate and help us to act in making positive changes while other indicators will not resonate so much; do not get over serious and worry about whatever insight you gain.

Make Changes in Your Life Checklist Notes

Noise

_____
_____
_____
_____
_____
_____

Change

_____
_____
_____
_____
_____
_____
_____

Challenge

_____
_____
_____
_____
_____
_____
_____

Make Changes in Your Life Checklist Notes

Outside Influences

_____
_____
_____
_____
_____
_____
_____
_____
_____
_____

Inside Influences

_____
_____
_____
_____
_____
_____
_____
_____
_____
_____
_____

The practice

_____

_____

_____

_____

_____

_____

_____

_____

_____

_____

_____

_____

_____

_____

_____

_____

_____

_____

_____

_____

_____

_____

_____

_____

_____

XII

CREATING INNER AND EXTERNAL SPACE

First, we must begin to create space between the noise and our own self by identifying where the noise is coming from and how can we create quiet and alone time for our own self, affectionately called "me time." Identifying the opportunities to create external space and time when we can remove our self from the noise will be vital. Once identified, we can begin to plan when take advantage of that external quiet time and space.

At the same time, we must look at our own self and our own schedules to see if we can utilize that space and time to enjoy quiet time. This time is utilized to become calm, centered, relaxed, and peaceful, without breaking the appointments we have with all the tasks that need to be completed on a daily basis. This is crucial because, when creating an environment in which we can take advantage of relaxing, we have to allow our self to do exactly that without sabotaging with excuses. For example, saying such things as, "I am not ready," "I am scared," "I cannot do it because I will not allow myself to do it," "It cannot be done," or "I'm too busy." These excuses must be trivialized and pushed out of the way to reach our goal and achieve the inner peace we deserve. It is like that piece of fudge you have been dreaming about. It is like a decadent cheesecake you have been wanting. A slice of each brings happiness to the mind; you cannot be satisfied until you get a slice and take that first bite.

Know Balance

What is it that we really need to know in this life of ours? We need to know our own self, with its pros and cons, strengths and weaknesses, dreams and goals, motivations and urgings, and needs and wants, to name a few. We also need to know, most importantly, our own hearts and minds to understand why we are who we are. We need to understand our health and wellbeing; then we can evaluate our own life and our current situations or present moments. We need to remember the present moment is all we have in totality. It means that, wherever we are or wherever we go, we bring our self completely, and we do not need to bring anything else. Because you are who you are then, you can be present within yourself when you breathe, move, talk, listen, meditate, pray, eat, and sleep. Why is this relevant? Often, we equate our lives with that which we cannot carry; we equate our lives with others that are apart from ourselves, or situations that we feel we are controlling or are controlling us. Once we reach a place of presence in the moment, then we can focus on ourselves, on our minds, our hearts, and our little pieces of the universe: the microcosm of whom we are. Then, we can know our peace without denying it exists and begin to settle in the center of our being. Once this is done, then we are home and ready to balance.

Balance

Balance is where we want to be within our own self, first, and then we can see the balance in the outside. Balance in life gives us the ability to ensure that we have a total life, and that all we do is a part of that; but it is all in equilibrium and that is where we want to be balanced. Our hearts can then see straight, we can be centered, and we can know where we are in that moment. The juggler balances the balls or pins he is throwing up in the air. Scales of justice suggest balance even though we question the truth. Even if it does not, we always hope it will. We hear many say that they work hard and play hard; this is to suggest that is their balance. We can then articulate our minds, our hearts, and our centeredness, and know we are in a place of control, at peace, quiet, and with or without activity. When meditating or doing a walking meditation, we become calm, strong, and powerful, able to see the calm before the storm and know how to navigate the waves and ride them to shore.

Balance is the buoy of life that helps us to float over all that is brought to our front door, whether storms or calm waves, just as the surfer surfs the waves, large or small. The surfer has to be balanced in riding the surfboard and then balance the board on the waves. In our meditation we can just sit, center, breathe, and smile; for we are calm, balanced, and at peace.

In Conclusion

When we have created that external and internal space and time to begin to focus on oneself, we look forward to beginning to experience it; when having experienced it, like that double chocolate slice of cake, we want more and will try to ensure we have more "me time." We will enjoy relaxing and appreciate the calm space and time that we have allowed on our own behalf. Of course, this will be a process, and it will take time for us to become comfortable and able to enjoy our ability to relax, be calm, and to develop and experience the joy of inner peace. Balancing ourselves is a requirement, no matter where we are or what we are doing or dealing with at any given moment. We only have ourselves now and we want to present all of whom we are with our inherent power to handle and control oneself.

One must obtain balance on some level in order to obtain peace within, so meditate on balance. Check to see what is in and out of balance. Begin to aspire for balance. For example, the phrase "all work and no play" is not healthy for you and vice versa; "all play and no work" speaks to us on balancing life. These are only a couple of examples, as there are many more.

Exercise 1

1. Write down on a piece of paper your strengths and weaknesses, dreams and goals, motivations and urgings, needs and wants, and what you think or feel is in your own heart and mind.
2. Then, on the other side of the paper, write down what you love, what you love to see happen, what you can do to change anything you do not like, and where you are now.

3. Lastly, what will make us feel in balance now, not yesterday or in the past, but at this very moment?
4. Evaluate what you have written down and determine what will create balance in your life.

Remember what will make you feel in balance every day and put it into action. **Be happy in the present moment** knowing you are you, with love, and moving to a state of balance, if you are not already there!

XIII

PEACE, NOWHERE IS THE PROBLEM AND THE OPPORTUNITY

I Sail the Seven Seas

I sail the seven seas
Only in search of my love
Only to find the seas teases
I pull out my oar
Wanting to chart to a familiar shore
But find the high tide and wind,
Blow me to a foreign soil
It feels like I have been here too more and more
Seems the seas control me more than it should
I figure it is for my own good
But a fool's paradise is strewn in the wind
And the shores of fun in the sun,
Shine more bright than
The moon at night
And I realize the sunrays are the way
That lights my path by day,
Revealing all the chatter and stuff that supposed to matter
But I seek the peace as I travel at night
provided by the moon's bright light
for only I am looking for my love
on the seven seas
like a kite flying to new heights
new shores, new sights, new waves
New battles to fight
Or am I searching for me
Or looking for peace?

We look for peace in our immediate environment and, for many, peace is to be found nowhere. The TV does not provide any. The government does not guarantee any peace, and it does not support peace. Since government officials spend most of their time creating havoc, wars, and disingenuous environments, while proliferating dissension among people and communities throughout the country. Universities are no better, and religious organizations do not bring the masses together to foster peace but to advance instead their own agendas, whatever they may be. Mistrust and division are everywhere, and the teaching of hate and war do not invite peace amongst the masses of people who only look to be in an environment of peace and happiness. Negativity is around us, and we have to remain positive and develop our own peace, no matter what is transpiring outside of us; we must try not to allow it to infiltrate our own being.

For those who have been taught hate and divisiveness as a way of being and dealing within their own situations, it is important to release it and understand the adages "live and let live" and "love thy neighbor." These phrases are guides for living within your community and dealing with all those we interact with on a daily basis. Hoping they support the same notions, then we, too, can relax and be calm, instead of living in the adversarial environment many of us experience every day.

Many may complain, but it is not time to complain. It is time to think happy thoughts and trust ourselves to be able to change and create a sense of calm and peace within our busy lives. We wonder why the busy rich executive will get up, walk out of their office, their secure job, and move to the farm. It is only for the peace, the calm, and the balance that they are now seeking this as their goal.

In Conclusion

Despite there being no peace in our environment and the government not advocating for peace, we should still do what is best for our own selves by stopping the promotion of hate and divisiveness. We must rise above our own thinking and know the government does not create peace; we do. Do not abdicate your own ability to be at peace. Violence is on TV and in video games, and it does not promote peace. We are required to seek our own inner peace. You cannot buy peace, but you can become calm and develop inner peace. Later, you can assist others. Wars do not create or bring peace; peaceful people create and promote peace.

XIV

WORK OF INNER PEACE

Ignore the Obvious

Ignore what people say you cannot do to remove the noise or the nonsense. Stick to saying, "I can do it," because only you can do for you, and only you can create your own happiness and be at peace. Being at peace is for you, and it is all about your self; although, others will also benefit from you being at peace. However, you will witness that later. The initial and overwhelming benefit is only for you. The ability to ignore the obvious is part of you beginning to become calm and develop inner peace. When you begin to ignore the noise and nonsense and you are not drawn to it, you focus on being centered and calm. Even though you observe the noise, you will not jump at the opportunity to become a part of it. Distractions are all around us, but centeredness helps us not to be so easily distracted, and we then can focus more on our center as opposed to extraneous noise trying to draw us to the sidelines.

Heart of the Matter

The heart is quite involved with the mind, and, in many cases, they work together to assist you in achieving your goals in life. The heart wants you to be happy, calm, peaceful, and full of love. Sometimes, we forget this and place things in the way that are not completely in agreement with our heart, attributes, or goals. It is vital that we express what our heart wants to make us calm, happy, and peaceful, the opposite of hateful, stressed, tense, upset, and agitated. One other vital negative we have to release or avoid entertaining is grudges against others that we feel wronged us in some way, even if they did exactly that. This means we must "let it go," whatever the nonsense or noise is or was, and focus on the now. Holding grudges will not change anything that happened in the past, but "letting it go" will change us in the present moment and when we move forward.

As you open your heart to follow the above adages, you realize that it is important for you to follow the same adage so you can be at peace within your own heart. It is easy to ask the mind to relax, but the heart has to be calm and relaxed in order for the mind to become peaceful. Therefore, we understand there is a heart-mind connection, and we must center our heart as we focus our mind. We also must calm our mind from dealing with all that is in our immediate environment, including everyday duties and tasks that we accomplish to a high level of efficiency. When the heart is willing, the mind must begin to help and relax or create a time and space within which to relax and be calm and/or quiet.

The Struggle

Yes, you have many balls in the air like a juggler, but you are good at what you do and you know how to juggle everything going on in your life. One of those balls must include focusing on you and your needs. You can say it is too much, but you can handle more than you think you can, so do not give up. You will make sure that, no matter what you are struggling to do and manage on a daily basis, you also find time to focus on yourself. Include scheduling some "me time" to relax, be calm, and at peace.

As we become aware of all of this and our own self-needs, it will increase our awareness of the struggle that we now have to deal with. We can either affirm we are going to do this (including focusing on oneself), or give up without even trying. We will try this (calm and inner peace) for one day and if it does not work immediately and perfectly, like a cure-all, we might give up thinking it is too hard for us. We will opt out for the easy noise and discord that we deal with on a daily basis.

Many say and witness life to be a struggle, and, within those struggles, they have difficulty finding peace and tranquility amongst all the noise.

However, within those struggles are answers and insights to our own ability to mitigate peace. We must observe the opportunities to be quiet, listen to our mind, tell ourselves to relax and not think or overthink so much, and center ourselves in a way to remain calm, relaxed, and, eventually, at peace. If we are serious and work hard, we will begin to relax more, stay centered, and remain calm when others get easily upset over trivial things, no matter what is happening at any given moment.

The Solution

The solution is in front of you. You are the captain of your ship. You decide where to go and what you want or do not want to do. You control your own destiny and only you can stop it. Do not let the past stop you or your present situation. Begin one day at a time to reach your goals, gradually, until you see the results. Know what is in your heart and mind, and know you can control the outcome and, more importantly, the income. I can hear the noise, I can see and experience the nonsense, but also, I choose not only to recognize it but also to step out of it. Contribute by taking you own reins and begin to determine your own peace. Yes, you determine your own peace in the middle of the noise, in the middle of the crowd.

We determine what disturbs us in our heart and mind, and we can control the outcome. This means that one can try to disturb us, but only we can let it happen, decide not to be upset, and remain calm and relaxed. Do not spend time beating yourself up over past issues; just relax and focus on the present. Remember that water always seeks its own level, so calm is like water.

Doing Your Practice

Whether through meditation, yoga, t'ai chi ch'uan, prayer, or mantras, you must practice relaxing, being calm, and being at peace. All of these are essential tools to assist you in relaxing and focusing on oneself, turning inwardly and forcing you to look at yourself. It is also important to understand that you must commit to doing all you have agreed to and making your practice a daily and weekly event. Commitment is essential because every day you will come closer to your goal, and you will attain it if you stay committed and continually practice.

The Ancient Masters taught and wrote about the need to be calm, centered, and at peace, even though we live in a world where much is going on in our lives each day. All of the practices (meditation, yoga and t'ai chi ch'uan) are to assist us in cultivating inner peace, wellbeing, and longevity. These methods have been practiced for thousands of years and they will assist us on our quest to ensuring we can succeed and accomplish our goals.

Exercise 2

Here is a simple technique that can help you everyday. Sit in a quiet place, feet on the floor, hands open, palms up, resting on your lap, tell yourself to relax by counting to 100 slowly and each time you count think, "I am calm and relaxed even more." Image the whole body and mind relaxing including your breath. As you count feel yourself calming, becoming more relaxed. If there is anything bothering you (any negativity) for this moment release it and let it all go into the earth. By the time you reach one hundred, determine how you feel, if relaxed and calm or not. This is an exercise in being relaxed and calm. Practice until you can distinctly feel the difference being tense or relaxed, calm or agitated.

Exercise 3

The first step to learning to meditate is to learn how to become quiet and calm. The second step is how to become relaxed and to look inside as opposed to looking outside of you. To begin, sit still on a chair, with both feet on the floor or in a lotus position if you are flexible. Be sure you are comfortable, and relax, placing your palms facing up on your lap. Practice the exercise (2) above first if you can't become quiet. Close your eyes gently and breathe naturally. Remain quiet and if you can't listen to your breath. Think about nothing. At the end of your exercise reflect on whatever you sensed, or felt. Doing this for 15 minutes a day will help you relax and be calm and become more peaceful. This is only the beginning technique to meditate.

In Conclusion

The work of inner peace is a struggle and requires a lot of effort because we are constantly in the world dealing with everyday things. We cannot ignore the elephant in the room representing strife and turmoil, but we can dismiss the elephant, take hold of our reins, and determine how to chart our own boat into calm and peaceful waters. Yes, it is a struggle to look at ourselves and let go of what is not in our best interest of being in and maintaining a peaceful environment; but you can step up and ensure you have peace within your own heart and mind. You are in charge of you. You can become present, let go of the past noise, and look into your heart to become centered.

You are stronger than you think. You must remain strong, and if you feel overwhelmed seek advice or help because you deserve it and it still shows strength. Commit yourself to accomplishing your goals one day at a time. Ensure you have some "me time" to relax and be at peace, even if it is only for a short time. Practice the exercises above. When you relax or rest for a moment, you will be stronger. It will help to renew your energy, and it will help to inspire you onward in handling all you currently do.

XV

WHAT IS KEEPING YOU FROM YOUR GOAL OF ATTAINING INNER PEACE?

Are outside influences preventing you from achieving your goal? If so, you have to begin to control the outside influences in your life in order to determine if they are good or bad for you. Is the environment negative or positive around you? Is it controlling you, or are you controlling it? Answer these questions and make the adjustments required to be and continue staying in control. Do not give that up to others. Do not let any outside influences keep you from your goals; make the adjustments to ensure that you move quietly toward your goal without fanfare, and keep it to yourself as you quietly reach it. It is your goal, and you will notice your change; do not concern yourself if others notice or do not notice. Later on, you may have to share it with others who will enquire and seek the same assistance to reach a similar goal.

What's in Your Heart and Mind

Is what is in your heart preventing you from attaining your goal? Start to release anything that is negative or begrudging; all past issues that do not contribute to you being happy, positive, or peaceful. Think about your heart being calm, and, if it does not feel that way, question yourself and seek advice as to what is going on. Part of this is being positive and truthful with yourself. It cannot all happen in one day or one month, but it will happen if you keep thinking positive and moving forward gradually. Become more heart-centered so that you can be much calmer, and this will assist your mind in becoming calmer.

What appears in your mind when you try to be calm and relax?

Think about what makes you calm and relaxed; then think about what makes you disheveled and upset. If you think of being calm and relaxed and, suddenly, something pops in your mind that from the past or present, fully focus on what it is so you can release it. Alternatively, deal with it or place it in a position that it will no longer upset you or unnerve your calm disposition.

Mindfulness

The mind is full of all that is going on within our lives and more, but that should not keep us from knowing what is going on within our own selves. Therefore, mindfulness is vital so that we know what we are doing, where we are and are not, and where we are going. This mindfulness is required so we can always be aware of what is going on instead of being on autopilot, causing us to react, not mindfully thinking about everything we think, say, or do. We will need to be at a level of mindfulness and knowing so we can accomplish our goals, including balancing all that we currently have to in order to deal with our busy lives. My mind focuses on peaceful and centeredness. What does your mind focus on? In addition, my mind focuses on everyday things such as bills and worldly issues, but they are secondary to my inner focus on centeredness, peacefulness, and love. We all focus our minds on whatever we choose or do not choose, but we can be mindful of what we focus on, and we can change to focus more on what we consider important at any moment.

In Conclusion

Often, we have to evaluate what we do and how we interact with others in different types of situations; but we can choose how to handle our own self in relation to whatever is happening or what we are dealing with at a moment in time. Be mindful of what you focus on, what is in your mind, and what is important for you to focus on. Determine if it is an inner or an outer focus or a combination of both. What we focus on is major, whether bills, health, money, hate, peace, and or love, so be mindful of it.

XVI

The Attainment

Every Day to Every Moment

Attainment is not instantaneous but requires you to begin a process of learning about you and how you react to all you deal with in the world. This includes your home, your community, while at work or at play, and they help you realize you can handle all you need to and still remain calm, somewhat relaxed, and be at peace if you make that decision. This goal is no different from any other, but it helps us to know our own self in all situations, learn to control ourselves in a way that, no matter what we have to deal with, we can be calm, relaxed, and attain a level of inner peace as we move towards our goal of happiness.

This attainment will affect your outlook and your consciousness as it begins to change and reflect on the inner transformation you are making. This change in consciousness is part of who you are, and it is a positive step toward expressing you, your heart, and you mind in a way that shows you are on the path to inner peace. As you commit to the changes and show that you are serious, your consciousness will continue to express a calm demeanor and you will feel at peace. You then will realize that you are all right. This is imperative because, at times, we question whether this is the right thing that we are doing. You question if you are all right as things change. Your perspective begins to affect your view of all that is around you, and, as you tone down the noise, you may think something is wrong. You may think that, because you are becoming calm or struggling to be peaceful, there is something wrong; but nothing is wrong.

Remember throughout this process that you are all right. This is important because we must not be so critical in thinking something or everything is wrong; we must begin to question what is wrong with you. Instead, continue to affirm that you are all right will be all right throughout the process. One more imperative is not to beat yourself up with questions of why you did not do this, years ago. The past is the past, focus only on the present time, and look positively to the future with a smile that you are all right! Life is about change, and positive change is part of our journey on the path to inner peace and success.

Adapting to Change

The life of change and the quest for inner peace are real in our lifetime, and we should seek it on our way to happiness. We sometimes like noise, but we also should like peace and quiet just as much as we like both waves and a calm sea. As we struggle, we must see the calm, we must let go of the stress and tension in our lives, and we must have a place to relax. Being overstressed and agitated all the time do not help us accomplish anything, and they do not help our health. Being upset all the time is one habit we need to break. Yes, it will require some additional management of our daily lives and all we deal with. It will also help us to un-complicate our daily endeavors and help us to realize we can achieve balance through relaxation and peace. In addition, we can learn to be calm inside most of the time, no matter what is happening or whatever we are experiencing. As we begin the process of inner peace, we realize that peace is all around us. We can take time for ourselves, just as we make time for others.

Realization

When you reach that plateau of inner peace, you will know and realize you have preserved and made it to your goal. You probably will celebrate inwardly knowing things have changed, even if it is only a subtle change, yet you will feel the goal reached was worth it. Once one realizes the need for calm, quiet, and peace, then you will begin to adapt to that change in your lifestyle. The "Aha" experience helps to verify whether we made the right decisions, and now we will have to continue to make sure these changes are implemented on a more permanent level. The spiritual journey many of you are on requires the accomplishment of many tasks; one of them is to become centered in the heart, stay relaxed, become calmer, and to avoid responding to all external and internal stimuli so that you can become more at peace.

In Conclusion

Affirm that I can choose to remain calm inside, even though outside issues are taking place at the same time. Affirm that I can choose to stay centered and calm, even though I have some internal problems or stressful situations, such as bills, lack of money, other people bothering me for no reason, a tire in my car blowing off, missing my train, or having to go through the TSA at the airport.

Meditation is another requirement that encourages us to become quieter and calmer, and it will assist us to be more at peace within. On the road to enlightenment, we must become quiet, calm, at peace inwardly, and realize we can be centered and eventually achieve inner peace. This achievement will be the result of changes we have made within our self, and it will affect the external environment and how we interact. Realize you have changed and are at peace.

Water

(Poem from my book, Lovers Should Never Quarrel)

Drink a drink of water my dear
Let the water course through your veins
Then let it flow through your body
As it flows let it show you the way
The water flows through you like,
The river that flows through the Ganges
As the Ganges flows through you
Your mind reminds you of ancient Egypt
As the water empties into the Nile
Visions of Cleopatra appear
You feel like Imhotep
And you rise up inside
For the power of the ancients
Are inside of you,
The light in you sparkles
Off of the drops on your lips
As it dips across the Great Divide
You take another sip
A sip so great
Noah readies the Ark
Knowing it is coming
But not worried for it will just pass by
Knowledge flows into your arteries
As your heart is filled with vitality
And once again you remember
Moses parted the sea at the Supremes' request
You think I too will save the
People from all the dread
From the drought
And I will thirst no more
For I have seen what this all is for
And your mind tastes

A taste of clarity
Of water's utility
And you realize
You don't want to waste
Another drop
Pollute another river
For you have seen Niagara Falls
And bowed before Victoria Falls
As you row thru the Serengeti
The Plains of Georgia have nothing on you
And even though it's hot in ATL
You thirst no more
For the crystal blue water
Has entered into your Spring
As it seeks its own level
Calm and peaceful
Quiet is the calm
Before the storm but
For now the sword of great fuss
Has been laid to rest
And all you can think of
Is my thirst has been quenched
And I can take a rest!

XVII

CALM IS THE WATER

When to be Calm and Peaceful

Power is the water and calm is the water. Calm is about peace. Relaxation is attaining the ability to be calm, even in stressful situations, and reaching a level of being at peace. As we move toward attainment, we will notice the high wave and the undertow trying to pull us into situations that want to upset our calm. The riptides will no longer have the effect that they did in the past. Those who thrive or strive on noise and altercations will realize we will not jump at the chance to create havoc, and they will notice our quiet, calm, and peaceful demeanor. The waters will come and go like the tide, but the waves will be calmer until we become like the still, calm sea. We can be at peace inside, even if we are around situations and environments that encourage us to betray our goals.

Cultivate the Diamond

Yes, cultivate the diamond. Curiously, you may ask yourself, "Where is the diamond?" Understand that you are the diamond. The diamond is within you and all you have to do is polish it and let it shine. Inner peace is like having a shining diamond in your heart, and you are calm and peaceful because you know it is there.

Sometimes, we cloud the diamond with things that does not matter or clutter we collect that causes oceans of emotion and inner turmoil. We can change that by understanding, within, we have the same ability to be calm and at peace. It takes effort to realize the inner emotional turmoil, ensure we will be and remain calm as well as centered, and instill peace within our hearts, minds, and beings. As we clear away the tension and stress and focus on our own diamond, we begin to rub it to shine within us. We then make sure that it stays centered within as we move from that center calmly and return in order to be at peace. Our diamond shines when we are at peace, in a sea of tranquility, and it shows on our face and in our hearts. Then, the smile appears within our heart and we know.

In Conclusion

What is in our hearts and minds will appear on our faces and bodies. So, are you exhibiting pain, suffering, hate, anger, and rage? Or, are you exhibiting light, love, inner peace, and happiness? For what you have inside (your heart and mind) will surely come out so others can witness eventually. Are you shining like the diamond you are? Or, are you unpolished and need to shine? If so, you need to look no further than your own heart and mind to determine what needs to happen. Just look within, check the balance, and, if not in balance, correct it with the secret ingredient called love. Yes, now you know. Balance yourself with love. Place love everywhere in your life within and without (outside). Love will prevail, and love is a place where your life needs to be, at a balancing point. Then, you are at your place of power, pointed in the direction of peace, which is within. Think of love, be in love, go forth knowing your heart is full of love, and all will know openly or silently; but they will see and know you are balanced by love, which will offset all issues you are dealing with. Placing a brick on the scale will not help, but love will, which is more powerful. Then, think "one love" as you journey to wherever you travel. The diamond will then polish itself until it shines brightly, not only in your heart but also around those you love and those that love you!

Tortoise of Longevity

XVIII

LONGEVITY REQUIRES

One of the factors determining longevity is the ability to relax, release stress, remain in control, and eliminate excess tension and anxiety in our lives. This is done, by practicing calmness, remaining centered, and staying relaxed in the face of all that transpires around us. Dramas that are transpiring and that pertain to us directly or indirectly have nothing to do with us; but they affect the community and our local environment. No matter how distant or obscure the drama, we must practice calmness and peace even more. The waves of interactions and drama we witness every day try to drag us into the midst of the sea of temporal things that will un-center us if we let them. At the same time, we must relax and remain calm, even as the world tries to involve all of us in its turmoil, which passes by us if we let it, like ships in the night. We do not have to jump aboard only to be stressed and upset at the things we do not understand or are concerned about. This drama is part of the incessant acting up and out, that plagues the many who also seek to be calm and centered and at peace, but who give it up for the lights, action, cameras, and noise, wanting to star in those one-act plays. We can watch from the sidelines, unmoved from our center, remaining calm, relaxed, and at peace to enjoy the light of the universe that continues to shine no matter what is happening on the ground each and every hour of the day. Relax because tomorrow there will be more, but our calm and peace is now and as long as we want it to be.

Longevity requires us to try to control the sway of the raging waters outside and within to become calm and even more peaceful. This will assist our energy and our resolve in preserving the inner peace we have so wisely developed and now enjoy. This is why the old Masters went to the mountain and the caves: so that their peace could not be easily disturbed by the passing noise and interruption.

In Conclusion

We do not have to go to the cave or climb the highest mountain to be calm and at peace. All we have to understand is that the mountain is within; we can sit there, on top, calm, centered, and at peace, even as we move and exist wherever we are. The road is in front of us, and we can see the calm, the sun shining, as the peaceful water of life flows to and fro, leading us ever happily on our journey.

Many elders or ancient peoples live to ripe old ages; they all have the ability not to suffer from tension and stress. They are able to remain calm and peaceful, even though they may not have all the riches or all the modern toys others enjoy. They are relatively peaceful with what they do have and are happy with their life. The reason is that the enjoyment and happiness are within, and so is the calm and inner peace. Longevity is not only in the food you eat or in the exercise, but it is also in the stress, tension, and anxiety you release.

Good luck and remember the goal is in the journey and success is on the path, no matter how high we reach. We are able to ride the waves, which have little effect on our being; calm is the water around us. Finally, let inner peace become your lifestyle, even while you are out there accomplishing the impossible every day. Do not forget to smile, knowing you are at peace!

Calm is the Water

Calm is the water
Tide is the way it comes in
Calm or raging
Tide is the way it must go out
Without a doubt
Rockin and rollin
Never staying put
We look and hope
There is no rage
No high waves
Covering up the storm
Hiding the hurricane
Like curtains cover the windowpane

We look to see what time it is
Can we take a dip
Or a sip
Is anything pulling us out
Of our comfort zone
Is there a play upon words or waves
Is the night hiding the storm
Will the light reveal the calm
Ripples tell the truth
If it is calm

Peaceful in my mind
I listen carefully for the noise
And the rumble as the calm sneaks in
Envelops my feet
As I sigh a sound of relief
I am happy
And at inner peace
No more am I calm sort of
I am now calm as water!

NOTES

NOTES